The Respect They Deserve...

Isn't about time we gave the respect back to our native insects, their environments, and homes?

For well over two hundred years our insects have been in their personal fight to survive. They don't have a voice, they cannot shout, scream, and make a noise when their homes are destroyed, the only sign they give, is when they no longer exist...!

The emphasis for the 2023 Chelsea Flower Show was on native fields and meadow flowers and grasses, and how refreshing to see the abundance of differently coloured flowers, their shape, form, texture, and vibrancy; some petals glistened as the rays of sunshine caught their movement in the soft spring breeze, and what a treat for any human being to enjoy the moments of this year's Chelsea Flower Show...!

They Want to Survive…

The butterfly you see, has many jobs to do, not only the will to survive but to pollenate the flowers it visits but to make babies for next year too…!

Its time spent is only a few, with so many jobs, and soon, this beautiful creature will need to support the new…

So fragile its wings and glorious too, but delicate as fairy dust, and now too often, too few…!

The butterfly has many messages to give, for it is the story, the story to live…!

Like mothers, from nature we find, the will to produce their babies each year, and to do just that, they need to know the earth will be kind…!

For once the babies are new, the mum's job is done, its short life is lived, for its legacy it leaves, its babies for next year, the flowers it pollinates and the beauty it gives…!

When you see your next butterfly, please take the time to ponder, and then wonder, not only at the joy of the sight, but at the work it does with all its might….!

Content

	Page
Garden Displays	1
Show Gardens	2
Titled, 'A Letter from a Million Years Past…'	3
Coolness of Colour – The Myeloma Garden	5
The Natural Affinity Garden	7
Turning Rubbish to Treasure	9
Gracious and Cool	11
Daisies, Daisies, Daisies…	12
More Choices of Cost-Effective Garden Designs	13
The Magic of Space – Poem	16
The Great Pavilion	17
Expectations	18
Upside-Down Flowers…! The Yellow Brick Road	19
Soft and Demure	21
Cor-Ten – Popular and Different	22
Alliums Galore	25
Amaryllis Lilies	27
Rosies, Rosies, Rosies	29
Big Show – 'GOLD' Disbud Chrysanthemums	31
Daffodils & Narcissus – a Sign of Spring	33
Clematis – Pictures of Perfection	35
Picture of Perfection	37
The Night – Poem	38
Succulents and Cacti	39
The Magic of the Moment	41
Semi-Tropical Flowers	44
Trinidad and Tobago	47
Zantedeschia – Colours to Make Your Heart Sing	48
Incredible Orchids	50

If you have purchased this book without its cover, it may be a stolen book.

Neither the publisher or the author is under any obligation to provide professional services in anyway, legal, health or in any form which is related to this book, its contents advice or otherwise.

The law and practices vary from country to country and state to state.

If legal or professional information is required, the purchaser, or the reader should seek the information privately and best suited to their particular needs, and circumstances.

The author and publisher specifically disclaim any liability that may be incurred from the information within this book.

All rights reserved. No part of this book, including the interior design, images, cover design, diagrams, or any intellectual property (IP), icons and photographs may be reproduced or transmitted in any form by any means (electronic, photocopying, recording or otherwise) without the prior permission of the publisher. ©

Copyright© 2023 MSI Australia

All rights reserved.

ISBN: 978-06459403-7-4

Published by How2Books
Under licence from MSI Ltd, Australia
Company Registration No: 96963518255
NSW, Australia

See our website: www.how2books.com.au
Or contact by email: sales@how2books.com.au
Covers and Copyright owned by MSI, Australia

MSI acknowledges the author and images, text and photographs used in this book.

10% of the sale of each book helps to support Diabetes Type One and Cancer Research.

Welcome to Part Two –

The Magic of Chelsea -

A Flower Show Like No Other

Welcome to Part Two of 'The Magic of Chelsea. In this part we introduce you to the beautiful Show Gardens and give you ideas of how small spaces can be transformed. We also go inside the Great Pavilion to show you different flower displays, finishing up with the beautiful display of orchids.

There are many flower photographs for you to slowly go through and enjoy. The clematis are especially beautiful in this show, but so too, for succulent lovers are the displays of astonishing flowering succulents.

Please and love the moments of this beautiful book.

The Reason Why…?

Since 1804, the RHS Chelsea Flower Show, has been an annual event. Originally it was called The Great Spring Show.

In 1913, it was moved to its present location at the Royal Hospital, Chelsea.

It's the glamour and excitement that makes the flower show such an exciting event. It is the event in many people's calendars each year that allows the show to be the success it is in the twenty-first century.

The Royal Hospital, Chelsea, is home to about three hundred British Army veterans, which include both men and women, all of which call the hospital, 'Home'.

Many of the veterans have served in Cyprus, Northern Ireland, the Falklands War, and the Second World War, from (1939-1945).

Originally, and the precursor to the establishment of the hospital in 1677, it was established for officers of disbanded regiments, soldiers with injuries, which was the original force by Sir Stephen Fox (1627-1716). Royal patronage was added to the establishment by King Charles ll in 1682. The purpose of the hospital was to establish a retreat for war veterans.

The Reason Why…?

So many times, we see, the people that have served…
To keep our lands free…!

Through years of battle, we are here, not by chance you know, but by
dedication of the people we cannot see…!

The numbers too great to count, but sometimes we may reflect, on those past
lives that allow us to live our daily lives…
Though they may be humble, we are at least free…!

With the tradition we hold, those lives once lived, and may we not forget
the enormous price they paid…!

To allow us to make the choices we freely make as from day to day
We learn….

The wonders of the moments, some of the past veterans did not
have time to yearn…!

For this is the reason, that so many can enjoy, the wonders of the
Chelsea Show that so many have not had the time
to know…!

Many people want to see the wonders of the show, and
yet, it's time to stop, reflect, and the Reason Why
we know….!

In Remembrance.

Garden Displays

People love to look and experience the garden displays at the Chelsea Flower Show. People are given inspiration to work within their own gardens through the cleverness of the designs on display.

The incorporation of charity stands, and the good work that small groups within our communities are creating in allotments, small gardens, all of which are acting to bring people together. This may not have happened, if the idea for community involvement had not happened in the first place.

Show Gardens

With many gardens to visit and to board the plane the next day back to Australia, it literally became scarce moments spent at each display.

Having said that, we did manage to see everything that was of great interest to us.

The gardens at the show are always incredibly exciting and full of new ideas.

The Royal Entomological Society Garden opposite created a semi-dome of recycled steel and hexagonal glazing panels. The interior links a screen to microscopes which in turn provides a study space. With a direct purpose for study, the coloured glass, colours radiated from the sunlight, are a similar replica to the eye of an insect. This display was a fascination in construction and the use of materials for the study of insects.

The biodiverse planting attracts insects to the natural habitat created, thus, allowing them to pollinate and provide a year-round food supply and the follow-up interest of study.

Not seen, a flowing stream, and still pool, allows for the collection of water which supports a variety of insect life.

Titled, 'A Letter from a Million Years Past...'

This garden allows a little insight into how medicinal herbs grow and are harvested on Jirisan, the highest mountain on mainland Korea.

The open top of the building, seen in the larger photograph, herbs, once picked, this area is used for drying the herbs.

The creating of sustainable landscapes and environments, by Jihae Hwang, are viewed from a conceptual viewpoint, whilst having many ancient roots in practise and use. It is the environment and the use of natural materials that allows us to see this insight into the knowledge and understanding of how herbs grow and can be used to assist human health.

Having said that, it is not surprising to see this garden design and its message taken to the Chelsea Flower Show.

The use of natural, but muted colours, are part of the natural world, often with colour only coming into play at the right seasonal time of the year; such a time is dedicated to the plants or animals of that environment.

Many builders and building designers are slowly turning to natural earth products to build sustainable and thermally efficient homes which cut down on energy for heating and lighting, which in turn, supports the earth and the environment!

Coolness of Colour...
The Myeloma Garden

How many hues, tints, and shades of green are there in the natural world of vegetation?

It would be impossible to imagine the world without the colour green, and yet, somehow, when we are so very busy, we can miss this treasure.

Natural living green gives off extraordinary energy that supports health and wellbeing for all living things, including animals, insects, and human beings...!

As with all of nature's treasures, we should each enjoy the moments of these visual sensations.

Many people diagnosed with life threatening illnesses find a sanctuary in the garden, and so it is that Chris Bradshaw, has designed this festival of green representing The Myeloma Charity, United Kingdom.

Here we see seven, or maybe more green colours, which are interspersed with a touch of white and small splashes of blue...! When looking at the display, the feeling of tranquillity, peace and breathless sensation can overcome you as the colours throw their beauty out to their spectators.

The ferns are particularly interesting in their visual presentation, with light and shade playing its role as the different colours of the clouds above show the feather-like fronds, against the wider solid leaves seen opposite and below.

Just to throw our visual senses into disarray, the slight colouring of reddish-to-orange shows itself in the larger leaves seen in the photographs.

The Natural Affinity Garden

The coolness of this garden with the intermingling of some grey-green foliage, touches of Wedgewood blue, and the occasional whisp of white flowers leave an impression of coolness and charm; it is unequivocally, the coolness and softness of the traditional English garden.

This garden is composed of three main elements: trees, plants, and stone within three specific zones.

The plants have been specifically selected for the sensory qualities within each garden zone.

The zones are designed to stimulate the visitor's senses, and this supports the nurturing of individual wellbeing.

The garden design by Camellia Taylor, gives the visitor an insight

into how each of us rely on our senses to help us work, play, have time out and a time for relaxation.

As a teacher of psychology and having taught many different children and young adults with different needs, when understanding that our senses play major roles in our lives, it is the acknowledgement of the senses, that assists us to effectively manage different life situations.

In the photograph opposite, it is the soft touch of pink that shows the feeling of gentleness and ease of the plant placement.

The design is an acknowledgement to Aspens, the charity that provides quality care and support for people on the autism spectrum, and those with learning disabilities. The team at Aspens work to support, not only the young person but their families.

Aspens provides a rich environment that allows positive learning and growth, developing maturity and to increase each person's enrichment enabling them to take opportunities, as they increase, in their knowledge and wellbeing.

While the garden is full of sensory stimulation, the one element that allows for the grounding of the design are the rocks seen in the below photograph.

By introducing this stabilisation element, the rocks allow us to take visual time out and to mentally rest on the journey.

Proportionally, it is difficult to understand visual balance when in the creation stages of any design. Once construction is completed, it is only possible to see if the design has the visual balance necessary to make it acceptable and pleasing to the human eye.

This design was both extremely rewarding to look at, and most definitely added to our satisfaction of the day.

Turning Rubbish to Treasure

Recycle, reuse, and help to save the planet and the global environment.

Whilst we have gone through the Industrial Revolution, and many have benefited from the outcomes of the inventions of the time, it is time now to 'take stock' of the outcomes.

Recycling and reuse were very much the theme of the show. Not forgetting the other positive outcomes for our natural world insects, animals, and flora. By recycling, we will start in the beginning phases of allowing the planet to start to heal.

Having said that, in so many parts of the world, there are more homeless people, and they all need shelter.

This design was an interesting concept that left us thinking, 'how can

we in Australia and the United Kingdom, use more items to recycle them and use them in garden features? It is only a small step at this point, but something we all need to think about when thinking, 'we need a new shed…!' Or when something needs replacing in the garden such as garden furniture and other replacement items.

The pinnacle on the roof of this garden building was more a study in the use of different materials used to create interest within a garden setting…

The sloping roof structure had a mesh-type construction, with what appeared to be dried laurel leaves attached replacing either shingles or slate.

Many dried leaves such as magnolia, and some laurels, give the appearance of softly polished leather once they have been preserved in glycerine. The leaves could be misleading and may be cut from a form of metal. Regardless of the material used, it does show that many items can be recycled and used in garden constructions.

The interest in the roof design does not stop there, but looking deeper, one needs to follow the shape of curved pipes, possibly resembling growing vine stems, these may have been re-purposed to collect rainwater.

Such a garden building may become a place of relaxation and enjoyment.

Gracious and Cool...

As the warm afternoon sun hit the show, the tantalising coolness of this display was felt by many visitors.

We naturally realise that mosses are cool, but when seen within the context of a warm day, it does something to our minds, it seems almost out of character with the Centre of London location!

In this design, many different mosses were used to cover rocks and to give the feeling of an ancient landscape.

As singular cell plants, mosses offer an added advantage to the planet in the absorption of CO_2, while offering in return, clean air which enables all living creatures to survive.

With such an emphasis on natural and back to nature, and the natural environment, it takes us many light years away from the finely clipped lawns and the gardens of the sixties, seventies, and eighties...!

Daisies, Daisies, Daisies...

The singular beauty of a daisy patch in any garden conjures up the idea of a daisy circle in any person's mind, relates to fairies at the bottom of the garden, wishing wells and buttercups. And so, it is with natural wildflower gardens.

Sleepy sunny, summer afternoons and all the feeling of lazy days were present in this garden display. It presents stillness, sunshine, and a time to doze....!

A natural selection of summer flowers is easy to accept with the hustle and bustle of a busy show...

More Choices for Cost-Effective Garden Designs

With such a choice of design, and the use of many different building materials, it allows the human mind to go crazy. Used in the below design are concrete containers which give a strength to any garden display. Now, there are available, environmentally friendly concretes that are made from re-cycled materials. They leave no carbon footprint and make for healthy environments for both humans and animals.

The curved archway in the background allows us to look further and beyond the display. This is an interesting concept as it allows the garden to extend beyond its physical boundaries!

By using a bit of creative imagination, we can make even the most boring of backgrounds look interesting.

Imagine an old, shed wall that has been annoying since the house was bought, or since the house was renovated! Don't let those bricks go to waste, use them to make a feature in the garden…!

Or if there is somebody selling off wood end leftovers, all can contribute to 1, saving money, and 2, creating a tranquil and positive extra living space…!

Recycling and maximising used materials will all help in reducing waste, pollution, and the stress on the earth's wellbeing.

Opposite, the visual play of the wood cuts left in their natural state glued against a deep-slate coloured wall, create an exceptional, extra living space, and contribute to an individual 'peace of mind'.

The Platform Garden, can give many ideas for revamping an old garden shed, wall, or simply create a space that you can use in different ways. Once making your decision the outcomes can be miraculous…!

In the opposite photograph, green tiles, which I remember being on the walls of the underground tube in London, when I was a child, are now a fashion statement. Green is traditionally recognised as a growth colour, so for the 21st Century, it is visually, very acceptable.

In this setting, and as you can see, the ground covering is cement, but if planter tubs are placed strategically, even unsightly surfaces can become glamorous and inviting…!

Opposite, large beams of wood created into an 'open air' outside room, can make an extraordinarily inviting back garden room which can be perfect for 'working from home' on a summer afternoon or while taking a tea or coffee break.

So many more liveable outside spaces are being produced by people being creative for either found or re-cycled materials.

The Magic of Space...

We had this little space you see – wasted it was, untidy too...!
something needed to be done and start from new...!

For much space we needed to have more fun –
books to read, articles to write and so much to be done,
without the traditional fight and created from none...
!
'You've taken my space...', we could hear them scream,
'You're just awful, I was sitting there...' and

So, it went on into the night....!
The yells and the screams and into the fight...!

At last peace, descends, the space was now clear...
we can sit and listen and now at least hear...!

For space is a premium, I can hear you all cheer...!
'Yes, in our house too, and only meant for just the few...!'

Sometimes, it's nice to sit and lament...
for precious times that are often spent...!

Crowds are more and people are many...
and so, it is, life's special times are forgotten,
if not given space or any...!

Life quickly passes, for that we all know...
and it's the time we need to go and to show...!

Experiences are plenty and good to recall, and it's,
the mind space needed, when into the fall...!

Heartaches come and endurance is needed,
for time will not tolerate if not heard the call...!

It is in the 'Magic of Space' that songs and books are written...
For the special times we wonder, we fall and are smitten....!

And so, the 'Magic of space' is often so rare, but the mind is always
working to find the space there...!

The Great Pavilion

Chelsea is a wonderful show case for spectators to see how different community groups are working together to create support and good for the society, and in turn, many people.

The Great Pavilion provides some marvellous insights into the world of horticulture, community togetherness and a mass of creative living colour that team-ship, when more than one mind, hard work and planning can achieve.

I have written much on how our great human minds are always up 'for the challenge' to create something different, something that leaves a lingering and lasting impression on others, and this show does just that in the Great Pavilion.

Expectations...

The Great Pavilion offers such a magnitude of surprises, it is always a highlight on the trip. Upon seeing for the first time, the green display below, offered solace and coolness to the visual senses on a warm, beautiful, early, English spring day.

The coolness offered is immediately felt, with many visitors stopping to take in the magnificence of the display.

The photograph does not do the depth, and the feeling the creative intelligence used, to bring the combination of living plants and static rocks together, justice.

The use of ancient ferns, so vital to the environment in this time of global warming, brings us again to the mosses that help to support and maintain a constant in, and stable healthy plant and animal existence, are all seen in this one display.

And, of course, it won a 'Gold' at the show...!

Upside-Down Flowers…!
The Yellow Brick Road…

How fascinating, such imagination…! Flowers hanging upside down and all looking as cheeky as ever…! The Yellow Brick Road, of course the name is taken from the film, Wizard of Oz.

This display by John Cullen, creates the world of magic and takes us into another dimension of interpretive design.

People stopped, laughed, pointed as they took the visual display back to their own memories of the film; such a clever way to bring a special day to the visitors, some of which, like us, had travelled thousands of miles to see such outstanding creations.

And from another angle, the Yellow Brick Road is clearly seen. Masses of flowers create this display with separate group placements of white alliums, which seem to appear in many displays this year.

Masses of achillea, 'Moon Dust' giving the yellowish to green overtone within the design.

Some achilleas, when in the budding stage, have a young greyish leaf and bud before the flowers and leaves mature into open

flowers. This aspect of the flower's growth can give a mist or ghostly appearance, which is fascinating to see as it blends into the overall design.

Different angles to the work give a perfect opportunity to see how magical the yellow brick road really is…!

Soft and Demure...

To blend soft pastel colours within any garden setting allows our minds to wonder, and goodness, in the times we are living through with wars, negative media, and so many people of the world wondering, 'what is held in the future for them and their families?' It's at these times, we all need some light mental relief.

A place to sit, look and marvel at the many flowers that are now in this 21st Century, and how many, if not millions of years, has it taken for us to look and wonder at these original and natural wonders that nature provides...?

Without too much thought, we can enjoy our natural wildflowers and cherish the seasons that bring forth the spectacles each year, such is the enchantment of the natural world.

Soft blending of colour, while allowing the natural formation of the foliage to have a voice, were all part of the appeal to this natural garden design.

Cor-ten – Popular and Different...

Weathering steel is seen on many newly erected buildings in both Australia and the United Kingdom.

In this display by the Birmingham City Council, and within its 'Free Parks for the People,' shows off the creativity of using an industrial steel material, such as Cor-ten in creative design.

There are the large tulips seen in the above picture, but when looking closer, there are three young characters pushing a hand-pushed lawnmower, and then looking even deeper there are cut from cor-ten, foxes playing within the flower beds.

Another of the features of this display include a large lily-shape flower which appears to be made from either platted cor-ten strands or from a hefty, dried vine of the same colour.

The abundance of colour allows the happiness of the event to come through and touch our feelings and emotions.

With so much to see and so much going on in such small surroundings, it's easy to forget about any concerns or problems we may have had!

It is not only the busyness of the event, but the effective use of space is remarkable. Just to stop and think, prior to about three weeks before the event opens, the grounds in front of The Royal Chelsea Hospital lovely down to lawns and flower borders. Within about a three-week period, the Chelsea Flower Show and its exhibits are slowly brought together.

The ground is dug, soil and lawns are removed, with all the exhibits in place, the show begins, and what a spectacle it is each year.

No two years have ever been the same, with new ideas for displays, different varieties of plants of all types and new flower types take their place at their display stands. And so it is, new materials are introduced, such as cor-ten, a commercial building product, that is now part of the garden and display scene.

The blending of the harsh steel with the delicate flowers on display, is almost in conflict but that too is what creative art is about. It is about using the ordinary to make the extraordinary, and by doing this, we can see how so many more materials can be used tastefully, and effectively, in garden, parks and large public areas.

Cor-ten is a sustainable material that allows rust to build on the exposed areas to the environment, the rust then acts as a protective coating to the steel.

The use of abundance and imagination helps to make the Birmingham City Council display as delightful as it was in 2022.

Alliums Galore...

To see the natural height of these magnificent plants, is itself pleasing but to see them in such quantities is nothing more than resplendent of the perseverance to develop beautiful flower specimens.

The looped stem and bud of the allium is novel and eye catching as seen in the side and lower photograph.

Alliums are a wonderful addition to the flower industry and the scope they offer in both traditional and modern flower arrangements.

These majestic and sculptured flower heads offer such an interest to the viewer and yet, they may hold the mystery of their own story!

Amaryllis Lilies

Amaryllis lilies were much admired by the Greeks and the flowers are mentioned in their mythology.

Going back to those ancient times, one can only again, be impressed, as the Greek population would have been at the delightful and sculptured shapes, the clearness of the colours and the lasting impression these flowers leave on our memories and emotions.

With their distinctive colours, the amaryllis lily is a popular garden and gift plant.

The plant is often associated with determination, love, and beauty.

Whilst amaryllis are often thought of as red, there are many other colours to choose from, and to melt our hearts.

These plants are often given as gifts or presents and symbolise to many people, new beginnings, which may reflect hard work and the determination to succeed with a chosen goal or achievement.

As a decorative flower, when teamed with alliums, they make striking modern flower arrangements that all people can achieve.

Surprisingly, the amaryllis lily is a distant relative to the asparagus family. The plant also has many health benefits including, it has anti-inflammatory benefits that reduce inflammation and ease body pain, it has antimicrobial properties, and has been used to heal wounds, cuts, and abrasions.

With so much to offer from the natural world, the amaryllis will be high on our shopping list for future gift buying.

Roses, Roses, Roses...

The beautiful rose blooms produced by the David Austin Nursery, never cease to impress the audience and spectators of the Show.

From stunning white to apricot and a great variety of pink blooms show us the achievement and beauty that can be achieved by perseverance and the love of the flowers.

To reach the pinnacles of perfection that was shown at this year's show can only leave the viewer feeling mentally replenished at seeing such a spectacle of achievement.

The perfume from the display was heaven sent and to say the least, it was an exquisite experience for just a few moments while enjoying the abundance of colour and headiness of the moment.

From single blooms to masses of showing combinations of colour, all was there for the audience to see and enjoy.

Roses have an ancient history and the love by all civilisations and generations who have had the pleasure of their beauty, never fades.

And so it was with this year's show of roses, colours, perfume, abundance and all of the ingredients that make the Show, the Show…!

Big Show – 'GOLD' Disbud Chrysanthemums

And what a Show…? Such magnificent blooms and the white were breathtaking at the first glance.

Of course, a Gold Award was deserved by such a magnificent show of these blooms.

These are again, an ancient bloom and kept in the gaze of the public by the enthusiasm of the growers and nurseries that cultivate and give us this visual feast.

The chrysanthemum was originally cultivated in China in the 15th Century BC.

Originally, being within the herb family, it was used for its medicinal purposes.

By 1630 AD 500 cultivars had been recorded. In 2014, it was estimated that there were up to or more than 20,000 cultivars throughout the world, with up to 7,000 in China.

Chrysanthemums have a royal attachment and are part of the Imperial Seal of Japan.

This magnificent flower is traditionally an autumn flower and associated with many ancient festivals in Japan. In Japanese culture, the bloom has its own symbolic day known as Chrysanthemum Day. There are several ancient festivals in autumn related to the bloom included the sacred festivals, one of which is held on the 9th day of the 9th month. This date coincides with the first day the Imperial Court held the first

Daffodils & Narcissus – A Sign of Spring...

Many people worldwide love daffodils or narcissus, they are indeed a beautiful flower in the springtime. Their colours are pure, perfume heavenly and the shape and texture of each bloom is crisp, sharp, and definite.

The people of the United Kingdom also love their daffodils, but they are native to Europe, the Middle East, and Africa.

The ancient Greeks also loved their daffodils and had the belief they brought good luck and joy; they too, used daffodils for home decoration, and adornment in the temples.

Daffodils are not an edible flower; they carry toxins in the yellow trumpet, petals, and bulbs; all parts of the plant have toxins.

The daffodil originated from the amaryllis lily.

Due to their popularity daffodils now come in a wide range of size, colour, and shapes.

Many of the old-fashioned daffodils had strong fragrances, and some are still enjoyed today; these include,
'Golden Spur,' 'Pheasant's Eye' and 'Early Louisiana.'

Clematis – Pictures Of Perfection...

Could there be anything more beautiful than the sun-kissed clematis on an early summer morning or when the dew has left its silver bubble to reflect the beauty of each single flower?

And so it is, and yet, another piece of nature's perfect creations.

Now, clematis comes in a range of different colours, to which all our different senses react.

From purples to vivid pinks, white, cream and back again to different hues of magenta.

Some of the clematis are scented, mainly in the climbing varieties. The deeply coloured purple clematis has a scent often released on a late summer afternoon when there is a degree of humidity in the air.

Scent differs between varieties, but Betty Corning is well known for the scent it has.

From miniature varieties to the larger flowers, all of which are stunningly beautiful.

From gentle, soft petal shapes to the intrinsically sophisticated centre of the flower, all of which add to the spectacle on display.

When the flowers are seen in mass proportions, it allows us to see the complexity and profusion of the creations.

With decadence of colour, perfume and excitement fills the air as these splendid specimens create their own majestic environment.

With numbers of people wanting to see these flowers and their plants, we were fortunate to capture these moments of splendour.

Picture of Perfection…

These displays will play with our memories for many years to come. The perfume will linger, and the thoughts will return….!

Clematis

The Night...

The evening scent fills the air, for flowers are letting you know they are there...!

Insects and night birds are waiting for the feast to begin, pollen and nectar to make their hearts sing....!

Flowers that thrive in the night, they are there and without any fright...!

Lavender, purple, pink, and white you may see...!
For the moonlight shines and twinkles on glistening petals
and flowers that are free...

Before the visitors start to arrive, first a late-night flying bee on his way home to the hive –
he stops for a feast and then on his journey, he goes on to strive....!

If you wait long enough you might see, late arrivals...
Such as the moth and firefly all wanting to find nectar and food to help them survive....!

The night swift may occasionally arrive, for it's the flowers high in the trees that are easier to find...

This allows them to feed with all who are kind....

And for many, they are safe in the trees, like bats who only feast at night, for all are needed and all need to eat without any fight....!

And so, it is, the night may be busier than the day, four our animals and insects we owe a great deal...!

Leave pesticides and chemicals out of the gardens and out of land fill...!

For once the creatures mentioned above, have little resistance to the fatal chemicals that make them ill, and many will not survive –
even if they are given a pill...!!!

Succulents and Cacti

Some people love them and some not so...!

I must admit, it has taken me many years to like these plants. I think the reason being, there are so many different and colourful types now, that they may even fit into the 'Cute' category of plants.

Most definitely, when these little gems start to show their flowers at different times of the year, they are very pleasing to have as indoor plants.

While in my training in floristry, one of my principal jobs was to look after the cacti...!

After their careful nurturing, I would spend the next week taking the small, barb-like hairs from my very sore fingers! Only to start the following week doing the same job...!

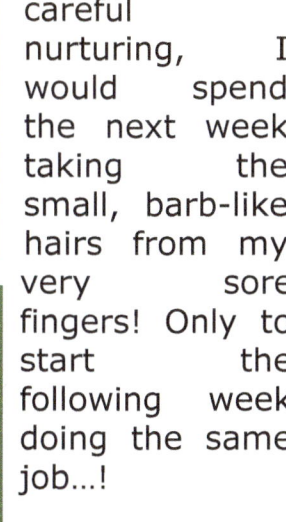

From those beginnings, the cacti and succulent families have come a long way. Now, such decorative plants, they make a talking point in many venues.

Showing so much colour, combinations, and difference, it is no wonder that people are now seeing these plants through different eyes.

The mesmerising balls of cotton wool opposite, would make an interesting focal point in a large modern home where the full complexity of their different beauty can be appreciated.

The appreciation of the succulent and cacti form, shape, texture, and the visual movement from one part of the plant to another, is, a study in time and patience.

A beautiful combination of plants made the spectacular displays this year.

The Magic of the Moment...

Combinations of texture, colour and movement can stop us in our tracks and this magical combination did just that. Here we see the different textures, amazing colours and plant shapes all playing a part in the different plantings within each display.

With rounded to spear-shapes, the different colours, and succulent types, these all work together to bring such visual delight to the array of plants now available.

Not only are there varied plants but succulents have the added advantage of giving unique and different types of flower displays at different times of the year.

Many succulents are affordable to begin collecting and seem to double up as they grow giving an abundance of colour, shape, and pleasure.

Many old containers that may collecting dust or put into the recycle bin for later use, can be used to make stunning indoor gardens that can be delightful all year round.

From many golden yellow colours to crimsons, whites and creams, these little gems can produce interesting displays.

In writing this information, I cannot forget to mention, it is the repetition of shape in many succulents that makes the plants so interesting to look at.

The display above and below allows us to see how the floret shape is repeated and repeated in the many individual potted plants seen.

The greyish plants can give an almost ghostly look, but when combining the plants together with other house plants, the interest they produce can be fascinating. If combining a grey coloured succulent with a pink cyclamen plant the textures, colour and shapes are splendid.

When a mass of cacti or succulents are seen in one space, the plants not only look spectacular, but they become a feast to see and study.

Watching the plants grow and enjoy their environment is not only good for them, but also good for us. We learn to stop, take a breath, and enjoy the time spent.

Plants in themselves are a therapy and help us slow down, take a moment, all of which help us towards good health and wellbeing.

Masses of shape, form, colour, and plants support the indulgence we see on these pages.

Semi-Tropical Flowers

I don't know if other florists or flower arrangers feel like I do, when I see a display such as the tropical flowers, interspersed with a few nerines, and other showy blooms, it makes me feel, *'I would love to have my secateurs with me now, I know I could do some magnificent floral displays...!'* However, that is not the reason we are attending this amazing show.

Jacques Amand has used delightful hot pinks of the ginger flowers through to flaming oranges and reds. Pulling the combination of colour and balance together, we see the leaves of the liquid amber in the photographs.

The magnificent leaves of the caladium plant, though a very large leaf combination is seen here, the size and colour of the leaves help to give visual strength, while picking up the hot pink tones of the nerines and ginger plants.

White allium towards the back of the design allows our eyes to travel slowly, without jolts, over such a striking combination and profusion of colour, texture, and magnificence.

Most leaf shapes are flat and therefore, make a positive contribution to flower design as most flowers are three dimensional and have a petal formation. By combining the different dimensions, and plains which allows the eye to easily move from one point of interest to another.

Positive leaf placements, allow floral design to become interesting and allows the viewer to become involved within the creation.

Below, the display presented by the Trinidad and Tobago delegation have created a beautiful and fascinating exhibit, showing different native flowers, vegetables and trees that grow on the islands.

Full use was made of the living materials used in the presentation with vibrancy, excitement, movement, and fascination built into the exhibit.

When we look at the different textures, shapes, vibrancy of the material used, it shows the commitment to giving the spectators a stunning and memorable experience.

Remembering all that is seen, with the worldwide expertise and competition shown by all exhibitors, this display has left its mark as a show piece.

Within tropical plant material, there are a great deal of different shapes and a serenade of colours not always seen in the traditional

of Northern Hemisphere floral and leaf material.

Ginger flowers, anthuriums, variegated foliage are all part of the cacophony of colour, shape, movement, excitement, and positive energy seen in these designs.

From falling and trailing vines, to vertical and straight, upward sweeping leaves, ferns, cascading throngs of orchids in upward spiralling movement all the design a poetry in motion of flowering plants and cut flowers.

Trinidad and Tobago

Masses of colour, vibrance and energy are seen in the Trinidad and Tobago floral exhibits.

Zantedeschia – Colours to Make Your Heart Sing...

Such amazing flowers, especially, when seen in great abundance as at the show.

The colours are sharp, but it is the shape of the flower that lends itself to modern and traditional flower arranging and in bridal work.

In bridal work, the stems can be left in length for a modern approach to wedding design, or they can be wired into place.

From a sharp sherbet-lemon colour to muted purple-to-lavender, and then to white or crushed strawberry, and then to the mystical colour of black to purple.

The variegated green to white lily is lovely but possibly much more common is the 'Green Goddess' arum lily, sometimes seen, regardless of the colour, the shape of both arum and Zantedeschia are magnificent flowers and ideal for the cut flower industry.

As many readers will realise, the lily shape is a bract or modified leaf, and we as flower arrangers, use these leaves in place of flowers in many designs.

Not only is the colour of these remarkable plants interesting to work with, but also when making full use of the leaves of the plant in all design work, this can add interest and visual momentum to any floral art piece of work.

Incredible Orchids...

Cymbidium orchids are incredible indoor plants. A good healthy plant gives a good number of flower spikes that are an ideal asset used in the flower industry. They can be used for bridal work, gift baskets and flower arranging in both modern and traditional design, but they also make good value when buying flowers for the home.

With such a generous display shown by the Orchid Society of Great Britain, there was a great deal to learn and appreciate.

The orchid, (Orchidaceous) plants are distinctive in consisting mostly of perennial, terrestrial or epiphytic herbs.[1]

The orchid that comes directly to mind, is the vanilla bean orchid, or 'V planifolia, grown for its commercial use. Having said that, there were many different orchids on the stand at this year's show.

---

[1] Epiphytic: orchids grow on another plant, especially one that is not parasitic which include: ferns, bromeliads, and air plants

Not only did the stand offer a good selection of plants on display, but so many different varieties not normally seen at the local garden centre or in local florist shops. That is understandable as many plants are rare, one in particular is the Caladenia discoidea, which is said to be 'the ultimate expression of floral deceit...'

These plants have developed their colouring and shape that lures insects to feast on the nectar they produce. 'Visual, tactile, or olfactory signals from the plant suggest the presence of a female insect. In some instances, the plant may ejaculate, thus adding to the confusion by the insects who visit it. That orchid is found in Australian terrestrial areas.

There are currently over 100,000 hybrids, and cultivars with 28,000 species of orchids found worldwide, and yet, there may be many more to be discovered...!

We know you have enjoyed this special book,
Part 3 is now available at your local bookstore
or directly from

www.how2books.com.au

Other Books That May Interest You

Available Online
www.how2books.com.au

The book, 'How To Create Easy Wedding Bouquets', introduces you to many techniques in wedding bouquet construction, the different methods used to wire different flowers and leaves, how to tape, ribboning the wedding bouquet handle, how to make a corsage, buttonhole and other industry techniques that will start you on a floristry career.

Our education company, Full Potential Education And Training has been developed to support people who want to learn how to build skills for the floristry industry. The course is a CPD Accredited 20-week online course in commercial floristry wedding bouquet making. It has been designed to support people who want to work for themselves and start a business or for those people who want a trade career in the floristry industry. For more information, please email, admin@fullpotentialtraining.com.au

The book, 'How To Create Easy Flower Arrangements', is an introduction to floral art and commercial floristry in flower arranging. The book is designed to help those people who want to learn flower arranging and construction techniques and will give the foundation knowledge to those people who want to work in the floristry industry.

It will also help people who want to learn flower arranging for pleasure and gift giving, and those people who create flower arrangements for special occasions.

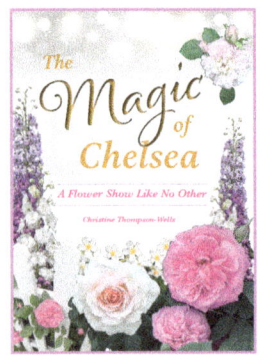 The Magic of Chelsea, 2022, is full of information covering the Chelsea Flower Show, floristry, art and design, sculpture, different plants and how they are used and has other informative and relevant information that gives the reader different information about the topics included. It would be an ideal book for florists, garden centres, nurseries and like businesses to have as a book for sale in their business. For wholesale information, please email: admin@booksforreadingonline.com

 Because we love the books we create, and poetry is a big part of the work we do, we could not help ourselves but include this book of different poetry.

 Without plants, we cannot survive. As all flower and lovers know, many plants and trees are under threat! Plants not only help to keep our planet and wildlife healthy, but they also add to our human wellbeing.

This book outlines the benefits of using herbs in our everyday lives. It is colourful and gives a breakdown of herb uses.

All the books are available at
www.how2books.com.au
This book is brought to you from the publishers of:

ISBN: 978-06459403-7-4

www.ingramcontent.com/pod-product-compliance
Lightning Source LLC
Chambersburg PA
CBHW041711290426
44109CB00028B/2848